EAST CROYDON

TO

THREE BRIDGES

Vic Mitchell and Keith Smith

Cover: A London Bridge to Brighton slow train on 17th March 1956 passes through Gatwick Racecourse station, now the site of the busy airport station. Designated 4 LAV, the train had only one lavatory, in the solitary 1st/3rd coach. The other three coaches had 3rd class compartments. (J.J. Smith)

Design – Deborah Goodridge

First published April 1988

ISBN 0 906520 53 3

© Middleton Press, 1988

Typeset by CitySet - Bosham 573270

Published by Middleton Press
        Easebourne Lane
        Midhurst, West Sussex
        GU29 9AZ
        ☎ (073 081) 3169

Printed & bound by Biddles Ltd,
        Guildford and Kings Lynn

CONTENTS

Map showing the main line electrification
in 1932-33. (Railway Magazine)

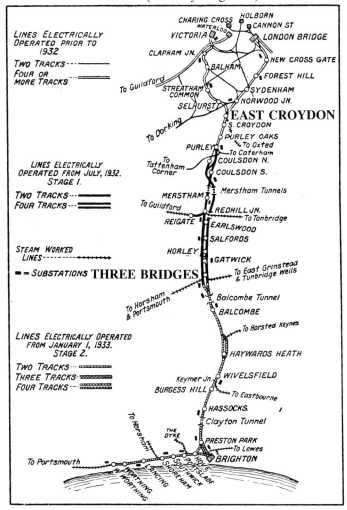

ACKNOWLEDGEMENTS

In addition to the photographers mentioned in the captions, we have also received help from J. Bradshaw, R.M. Casserley, C.R.L. Coles, Dr. T. Gough, A.C. Mott, J.S. Petley, R. Randell, R. Resch and E. Staff. We are very grateful to them and to D. Wallis and Mrs. M. Mason for permission to use the photographs taken by the late E. Wallis. As always, our wives have been of immense assistance.

GEOGRAPHICAL SETTING

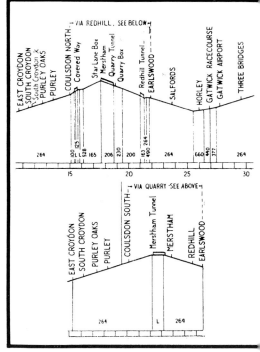

Croydon is situated on the gravels of the upper terraces of the Thames Valley. The railway route enters a valley in the dip slope of the North Downs and penetrates the scarp edge by means of Merstham Tunnel. On leaving the chalk, the line passes over a thin bed of Upper Greensand, followed by about ½ mile over Gault Clay, in the vicinity of Merstham. It then crosses deposits of Brick-earth on the Folkestone Beds, the sands in this area having economic importance.

At Redhill, the route passes through a gap in the gravelly Sandgate Beds to reach the relatively level Wealden Clay. Apart from an area of gravel around Horley, the remainder of the railway is on clay until gaining the Upper Tunbridge Wells Sands about a mile north of Three Bridges.

The North Downs give rise to a steady climb to Merstham Tunnel and their scarp slope gives a steeper fall to Redhill. The other geographical feature which affects the gradients is the River Mole, the headwaters of which cause the line to dip in the vicinity of Horley.

All the maps are to the scale of 25″ to 1 mile, unless otherwise stated, and where the route is shown horizontal on a page, the journey proceeds from right to left.

HISTORICAL BACKGROUND

The Surrey Iron Railway, between Croydon and Wandsworth, was in use between 1803 and 1846 carrying local goods, hauled by horses. In 1805 it joined the Croydon, Merstham and Godstone Railway, which opened that year to carry local produce, particularly lime. The line was never built south of Merstham. The wagons had flangeless wheels, the flanges being on the iron plates of the track.

The first conventional railway in the area was the London & Croydon Railway, which came into use on 5th June 1839, one terminus being on the site of the present West Croydon station and the other at London Bridge. The London & Brighton Railway Company obtained authority to build its line from a junction with the L&CR, a little to the north of Croydon, and to use its London Bridge station. The route was opened as far as Haywards Heath on 12th July 1841.

In the meantime, the Government changed its mind and ordered the South Eastern Railway to cease construction of its main line to Dover via Oxted and to build a branch from the L&BR at Reigate Junction (now Redhill). The L&BR were forced to sell this part of the main line to the SER and to share the line with the reluctant impostor. (MPs considered that one railway southwards from London would be sufficient). In 1846, the L&BR became the London Brighton & South Coast Railway and this company had to suffer the effects of a shared railway throughout its existence.

The SER route to Tonbridge came into use in 1842 and their westward extension to Dorking and Reading in 1849. Thus, Reigate Junction became the hub of the then SER empire and LBSCR trains were nothing but a nuisance to be delayed at every opportunity!

A branch to Caterham was opened in 1856 and operated by the SER from 1859. The SER completed a branch to Tattenham Corner in 1901. A joint line, with the LBSCR, was opened from South Croydon to Oxted on 10th March 1884.

The LBSCR opened a short branch from East Croydon to Croydon Central on 1st January 1868, to gain an advantage over the SER.

After suffering delays at Redhill for decades, the LBSCR decided to bypass the junction and constructed what is known as the Quarry Line. It came into use for freight trains on 5th November 1899 and for passenger services on 1st April 1900.

Electric services reached the route on 1st April 1925, when the overhead 1700 volt AC system was extended from Balham to Coulsdon North. This was converted to 660 volt DC conductor rail transmission on 17th June 1928. Main line services were electrified to Three Bridges on 17th July 1932 and on to Brighton on 1st January 1933.

PASSENGER SERVICES

The initial service on the route was six trains on weekdays and three on Sundays. By the mid 1850s, the number of Brighton trains had doubled and the SER were running six to Dover via Redhill.

The first timetable to include Croydon Central showed 12 stopping trains to and from London Bridge on weekdays, with three to the West End.

As the years passed the LBSCR service on the route improved while the SER made fewer changes, as their main line to Kent was, after 1868, via Sevenoaks.

Slip coaches were an interesting feature of late Victorian timetables. Between 1861 and 1879 down trains slipped coaches at Purley Junction and, from 1882, the 8.45 am from Brighton slipped a portion at East Croydon. At about this time, there were through trains to both Liverpool Street and Willesden Junction, in addition to the LBSCR and SER termini. In 1906 and 1907, even Paddington had a direct service to Brighton, calling at East Croydon.

By 1869, there were 13 trains running the full length of the route with 14 SER trains north of Red Hill Junction, as it was then still described.

As housing developments took place, service frequency increased, notably in the Purley area and at Horley, which also had the benefit of some slip coaches.

Initially, the Caterham branch produced no extra trains on the main line, as the junction layout prevented through running!

To give an example of Edwardian travel opportunities at Redhill in 1910, 18 LBSCR down trains called on weekdays, with 11 on Sundays. The SECR offered 23 and 7 services respectively.

Electrification to Coulsdon North brought a fairly frequent but irregular service which was changed to a regular 20 minute interval timetable with the introduction of conductor rail supply. Electrification through to Brighton and West Worthing on 1st January 1933 gave local passengers the best service ever. By 1938, Three Bridges had a minimum of one fast and two stopping trains to London every hour. Additional services, mainly at 30 minute intervals from Tattenham Corner, Purley and Coulsdon North, joined the route to give East Croydon a unique timetable to London. Trains were (and are) provided to every Southern terminus in London, if Waterloo East is considered as Waterloo.

The developing traffic at Gatwick Airport resulted in most trains from the West Sussex coast being diverted away from the Dorking route in 1978. May 1984 saw the introduction of the Gatwick Express to Victoria, the first air conditioned service on the Southern and running at ¼ hour intervals, daily.

An entire book could be written on the development of passenger services on the route but these paragraphs must end on another note of praise for BR. After an interval of over a decade, through trains to Manchester were reintroduced in 1979.

As we go to press, new cross-London services have been announced, for commencement in May 1988. They include Bedford-Brighton, Luton-Gatwick Airport and West Hampstead-Purley, via Crystal Palace.

EAST CROYDON

1. A Croydon Corporation tramcar passes the station soon after rebuilding had been completed in 1894. Until then it had been virtually two separate stations – road access to "New Croydon" terminus being where the shops are situated, the platforms having been added in 1862 for local services. The tram is fitted with a device to deflect jaywalkers. (Lens of Sutton)

2. The LNWR initiated a service between East Croydon and Willesden Junction in 1863. It ran via Clapham Junction and Addison Road (now Olympia) and was perpetuated by the LMS until 1939. Note the chimney mounted headcode. (Lens of Sutton)

3. A view of the south end of the station on 13th October 1915 shows repair work in progress following a Zeppelin raid. There is evidence of bomb damage to the footbridge pier. Students of signalling will observe South Box; a red painted distant arm with Coligny-Welch fishtail indicator and numerous miniature arms on the right. These indicated to fog signalmen when to place detonators on the running rail. (British Rail)

4. Trains are signalled on the down local and down relief lines as class B4 4–4–0 no. 53 arrives with a Victoria-Brighton service, in about 1921. A class D1 0–4–2T waits to depart north. Trains were frequently divided for Victoria and London Bridge at this time. (J.R.W. Kirkby collection)

5. The sign proclaims "East Croydon Main" on 18th December 1926. The western platforms were "Local" after the title "New" was dropped in 1909. Class E5 0–6–2T no. B405, formerly named *Fernhurst*, stands under the 6700 volt AC wires which were in use between 1925 and 1929. (H.C. Casserley)

2nd · SINGLE   SINGLE · 2nd

Three Bridges to
Three Bridges   Three Bridges
East Croydon   East Croydon
EAST CROYDON

(S)   3/-   FARE 3/-   (S)
For conditions see over For conditions see over

3055   3055

6. Looking south on platform 5 & 6 in June 1953, we see the loop from which the Post Office siding diverged. The track from platform 6 continued as a fifth line to South Croydon and was signalled for reversible running, after colour light signals were introduced in 1955. (D. Cullum)

7. The route to Coulsdon North was resignalled on 8th May 1955. This is the view from platform 3 on the previous day, with East Croydon South Box in the distance. Traffic was still on the increase – the population rose from 79,000 in 1881 to 252,000 in 1961. (D. Cullum)

8. After spending many years as a museum exhibit, GWR speed record holder *City of Truro* was overhauled and used on enthusiasts' specials. This excursion, on 11th May 1958, originated at Greenford and was taken on to Horsted Keynes by an ex-LBSCR K class 2–6–0. The Post Office siding is on the right. (S.W. Baker)

9. Electro-diesel no. 73131 propels the 14.20 from Gatwick Airport non-stop through platform 1 on 5th July 1984 as the driver in the motor luggage van at the front nears the 1955 signal box. This had been taken out of use on 7th April after which all signals were controlled from Three Bridges. The white bridge links the postal sorting office with the platforms – further major modernisations are due to commence in 1988. (J. Scrace)

A map and other views of this station are to be found in our *Victoria to East Croydon* album.

CENTRAL CROYDON

10. This long forgotten branch diverged opposite East Croydon South Box and was in use for passengers from 1st January 1868 until 1st December 1871 and again between 1st June 1886 and 1st January 1890. This 1923 photograph shows the connections which were retained until 1934. (Late E. Wallis)

The 1932 survey shows how the Fairfield Yard was developed. The sidings were used for engineering and building purposes until 1933.

11. The LBSCR scored over the SER by having its terminus for local trains close to Croydon High Street. After closure, the land was sold to the Corporation which erected a new town hall on the site.The present sunken gardens at the rear of it are on the position of the former approach lines. (Lens of Sutton)

12. The multi-vaulted canopy was similar to that provided at Worthing's second station, where part remains today. The luxury of two engine release roads was indulged in, but the turntable was near the junction.
(Lens of Sutton)

The 1870 edition gives the station the unofficial name of Katherine Street and shows its proximity to the High Street. The independent approach to New Croydon Station is also to be seen.

SOUTH CROYDON

13. Quadruple track between East and South Croydon was brought into use on 1st September 1865, the day on which the latter station opened. A Lewes bound freight rattles south behind class C2 no. 552, which was built by the Vulcan Foundry in 1902. (J.R.W. Kirkby collection)

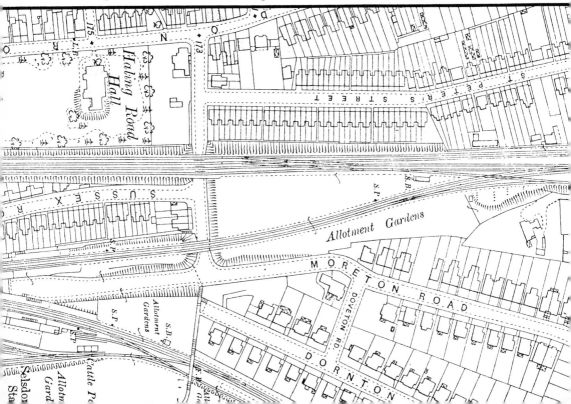

14. SECR H class 0–4–4T no. 295 approaches the station with a down train, while a class B1 speeds north with another SECR service. The two carriage sidings are on the right. (J.R.W. Kirkby collection)

The 1913 map shows the Oxted line diverging alongside the "Allotment Gardens" and part of Selsdon Road station in the bottom left hand corner.

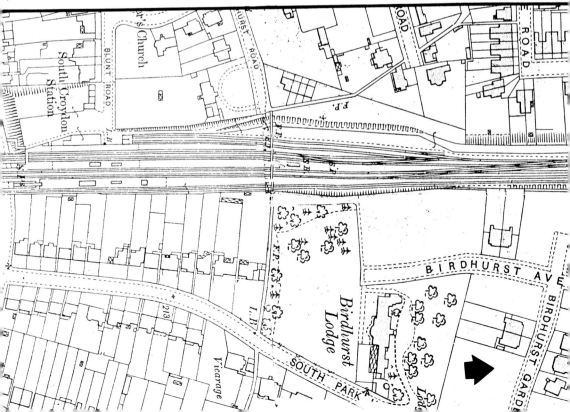

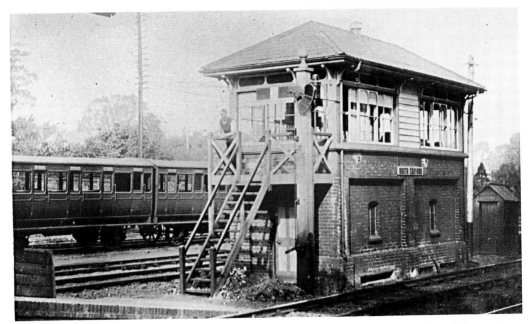

15. The 1865 signal box remained in use until 1955. In the carriage sidings of this much earlier view are two close-coupled 3rd class four-wheelers, which are devoid of compartment partitions. The signal post is of massive section. (Lens of Sutton)

16. A freight from the Oxted line passes through on the Up Main on 9th July 1963, headed by no. 31925, one of Maunsell's three cylindered class W 2–6–4Ts. The canopy on the left was erected in 1884 when other improvements were made associated with the opening of the line to Oxted and East Grinstead. This included provision of a subway. (J. Scrace)

17. This is the view from the 1955 signal box as a BR class 4 approaches the crossings before joining the electrified main line. In 1962 diesel electric units replaced steam on this route and were used until the line was eventually electrified to East Grinstead in October 1987. (Lens of Sutton)

18. From 1978 until the introduction of the Gatwick Express in 1984, twelve 4VEP units were marked "Rapid City Link Gatwick - London" and some seats were removed to give extra luggage space. They were then reclassified 4VEG. Unit 7901 leads an up train on 22nd July 1980, with the 1955 flat-roofed signal box visible in the background. It closed on 1st April 1984. (J. Scrace)

PURLEY OAKS

19. A down express, hauled by class I3 no. 77 and viewed from the north end of the island platform typifies the zenith of the LBSCR. The Westinghouse steam pump for the air brakes distinguished the railway from its neighbours. (E.R. Lacey collection)

→

21. The platforms were added on the main line in 1928, as can be seen in this 1937 southward view. From 1901, competition was felt from the electric tramway which was opened to Purley that year. The route closed in April 1951. A ballast siding was located near the houses on the right, in the early years of the century. (H.C. Casserley)

L. B. & S. C. RY
Available on the Date of issue ONLY
SEE CONDITIONS AT BACK
STOATS NEST for COULSDON & CANE HILL
[Local] TO [Local]
PURLEY OAKS
6d FIRST CLASS 6d

20. The station opened on 5th November 1899 with platforms on the local lines only. A substantial staff was required for an expanding passenger traffic and a busy signal box. (Lens of Sutton)

22. A northward view in 1954 shows economy in gas lighting and upper quadrant signalling, near the end of its life. The white diamonds indicted the presence of track circuiting or treadles and thus the need not to report to the signalman in the event of delay. (D. Cullum)

23. The extent of the generous canopies is evident in this view from the up local platform, again in 1954. The route south of South Croydon was quadrupled in 1899, when the Quarry Line was constructed. (D. Cullum)

24. The main buildings are on the up side and continued to serve their original purpose in 1988. The door on the right leads to the subway. (C. Hall)

PURLEY

25. One of the five original intermediate stations on the route, it was named "Godstone Road" until it was closed on 1st October 1847. The SER took control of the bankrupt Caterham Railway before it opened on 5th August 1856 but the LBSCR had to be taken to court to force them to re-open the station, which was known as "Caterham Junction" until 1st October 1888. This photograph dates from about 1890. (Pamlin Prints)

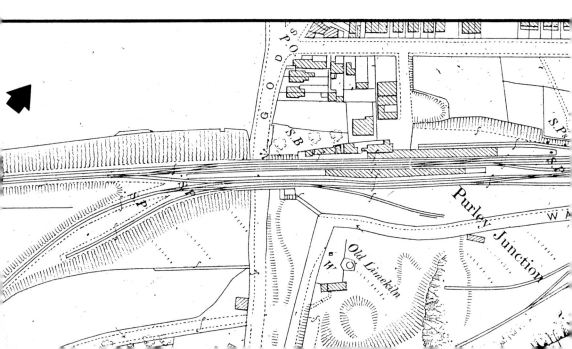

26. The station was totally rebuilt in 1898-99, as quadruple track was laid to link with the Quarry Line. Examples of the fine houses erected for the opulent are to be seen before all traces of the rural environment were obliterated by more season ticket holders. The crane is of 4½-ton capacity. (Lens of Sutton)

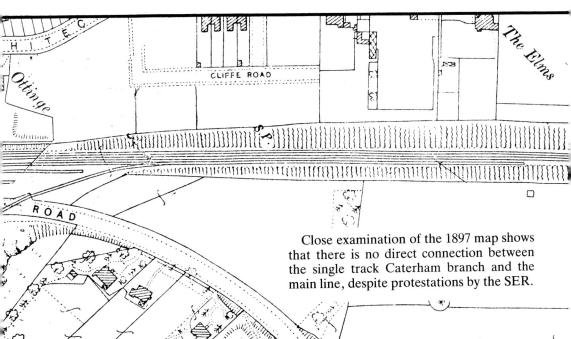

Close examination of the 1897 map shows that there is no direct connection between the single track Caterham branch and the main line, despite protestations by the SER.

27. As at Purley Oaks, the main building was provided on the up side to impress the city-bound travellers. The Chipstead Valley line was opened by the SER to Kingswood in 1897; to Tadworth & Walton on the Hill in 1900 and completed to Tattenham Corner in 1901. (Lens of Sutton)

The 1913 edition illustrates the far ranging changes that took place at the turn of the century. This includes double track on the Caterham and Chipstead Valley lines and provision of a goods yard in the former

28. Stroudley designed 2–2–2 *Stephenson* passes North Box in about 1912, conveying four Pullman cars on the "Eastbourne Sunday Limited". The goods yard connections can be examined in detail. (Lens of Sutton)

quarry. Four of the sidings remain in use – two for the engineers, one for coal and one for sand. General goods traffic ceased on 6th January 1969.

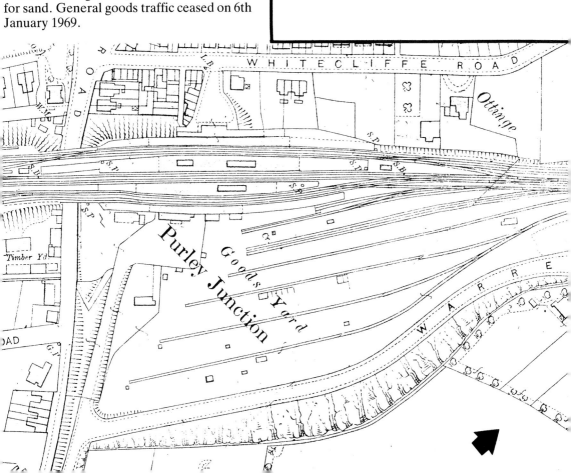

29. Six platforms and two signal boxes were provided at the time of rebuilding, North Box being visible in the distance. The platforms on the right were mainly used by branch line trains – the timbered part spans the road. (Lens of Sutton)

31. A southward view on 7th May 1955 shows the South Box on its last day of operation with the new box ready to replace both old ones. To the left of it is the roof of the former locomotive shed and further left is the electrical sub-station. The Tattenham Corner line runs between the two, before passing under the main lines, and the Caterham branch runs under the footbridge on the extreme left. (D. Cullum)

30. Despite electrification, there was still much to please the steam photographer on 2nd August 1926 as J class no. A129 departs for London and B2X class B210 proceeds south. For seven years, the SR used the prefix A on engines of Ashford origin and B on those from Brighton. (H.C. Casserley)

32. Looking from the new signal box in 1976, we notice that platform 4 has been extended and the direct connection to no.5 removed. Subsequently the extension was removed and the platform lengthened at the other end. In 1988, platform 6 was only used by two late evening trains, the former goods head shunt being used for stabling electric stock. (J. Scrace)

33. The locomotive shed remained standing in 1988, still bearing the inscription SER on the north end and 1898 on the south. On the right is the former SECR signal box, between the two branches. It was known as Purley East and was closed in 1928. In the foreground the Tattenham Corner line dips down before passing under the main lines, the position of which is shown by the catenary gantry. The shed was used by suburban locomotives until closure on 29th May 1928 and a 50ft. turntable was located at the south end of the yard. (D. Cullum collection)

COULSDON NORTH

34. On 5th November 1899, the LBSCR opened a new station with four platforms, two of which were on the new Quarry Line. The other two were used for terminating local services from London. The name was changed to "Coulsdon North & Smitham Downs" (the SECR had opened nearby Smitham in 1904) and to "Coulsdon West" on 9th July 1923, only to be changed back to "Coulsdon North" three weeks later. (Lens of Sutton)

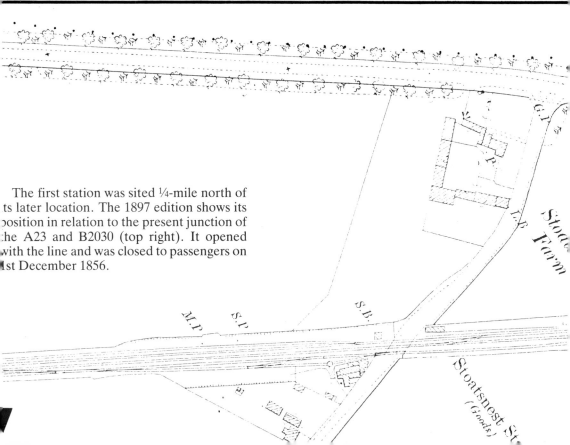

The first station was sited ¼-mile north of its later location. The 1897 edition shows its position in relation to the present junction of the A23 and B2030 (top right). It opened with the line and was closed to passengers on 1st December 1856.

Coal Yard

W.M.

S.B.

S.P.

S.P.

S.P.

M.P.

S.P.

S.P.

M.P.

S.P.

Allotment Gardens

Coal Yard

Limekilns

Old Limekiln

Scrub

317
1·572

Little
Stonyfield Shaw

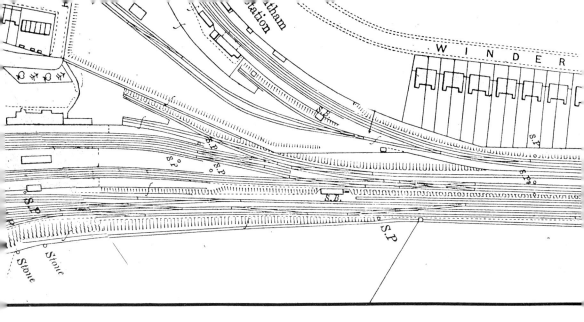

The 1912 survey emphasises the extent of Hall's quarry and the location of their lime-kilns. This map is almost continuous with the one shown for Coulsdon South.

35. The 3.40 pm fast train from Brighton was derailed approaching the station on 10th July 1909, due to a coach wheel moving in on its axle. The vehicle ran up the ramp of platform 4, turned over and seven fatalities were recorded, with 42 injured.
(E.R. Lacey collection)

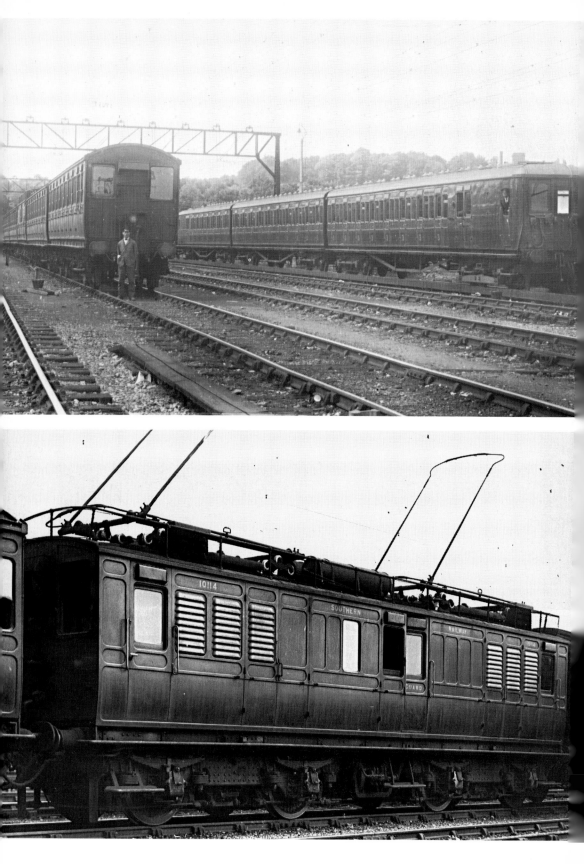

←

36. South of platforms 1 and 2, there were twelve carriage sidings which had both forms of electric supply in 1928-29. On the right is a 3-car set for the London Bridge conductor rail services which commenced on 17th June 1928. On the left are two 5-car sets of the type introduced in 1925 on the Sutton and Coulsdon North services. These continued to operate to Victoria until 21st September 1929. (O.J. Morris/E. Jackson collection)

38. Class H1 no. B40 *St. Catherines Point* speeds through platform 4 in 1932, bound for Brighton via the Quarry Line. By the rear coach is Coulsdon Central Box which was renamed North in 1937 and remained in use until 9th October 1983.
(J.R.W. Kirkby collection)

←

37. The middle vehicle of the 21 5-car sets was known as the "milk van", on account of its appearance but not function. The centre compartment was for the guard and luggage; this was flanked by electrical equipment and driving compartments were provided at each end. These were seldom used as the driver could operate from each end of the 5-car set. These 62-ton motor cars were converted to bogie brake vans after 1929. (H.C. Casserley)

39. "Live in Surrey and enjoy views like this from your windows". So ran the SR publicity message. The picture was taken from 22, The Grove, Coulsdon, on 6th June 1931 and shows the vaulted canopies of Coulsdon North station. The posters on the right are on Smitham Station.
(O.J. Morris/E.R. Lacey collection)

40. Looking south from platform 1, we see the Shunting Box, which controlled access to the carriage sidings beyond. The closed end of the locomotive shed abuts onto the end of platforms 2 and 3, on the left. (Lens of Sutton)

41. A 1954 view from the concrete footbridge which spanned the site shows the wall at the back of platform 4 on the right; next the connections between the old and new routes; then the old route to Redhill and finally Hall & Company's sidings to the chalk pit. (D. Cullum)

42. No. E6030 runs south on the Redhill line on 29th May 1968, the rear vans passing Coulsdon North Box. This was known as No. 1 Box until 1937. Smitham Box is on the

left, as are the platforms of Coulsdon North
station which closed on 1st October 1983,
along with the carriage sidings. (J. Scrace)

COULSDON SHED

43. Opened in 1900, the shed housed the engines for the LBSCR suburban services, of which these two class I1s were typical. There was also a small number of goods engines. This is the west elevation on 22nd August 1925. (H.C. Casserley)

44. A view from the south shows the massive water softening plant, added in 1911, and platform 1, on the extreme left. Part of the enormous chalk quarry is visible on the right, while no.B4 rests in the sun. The shed was closed in 1928 (J.R.W. Kirkby collection)

45. "Gladstone" class no. B619 passes No. 2 Box on 3rd March 1927 and was described as the last working of this class on a down boat train. No. 2 Box was closed on 2nd May 1937. Its position is shown on the map, near the connection between the locomotive shed and the Quarry Line.
(O.J. Morris/E.R. Lacey collection)

COULSDON SOUTH

46. Opened as "Coulsdon" on 1st October 1889, the suffix "Cane Hill" was added in 1896. This is the approach to the up side after the SECR was formed in 1899 but with the suffix omitted from the lamp glass. (E. Jackson collection)

The 1912 survey shows the extent of the goods yard, which was closed on 1st October 1931 as the Coulsdon North yard was so near. The tunnel is for the Quarry Line.

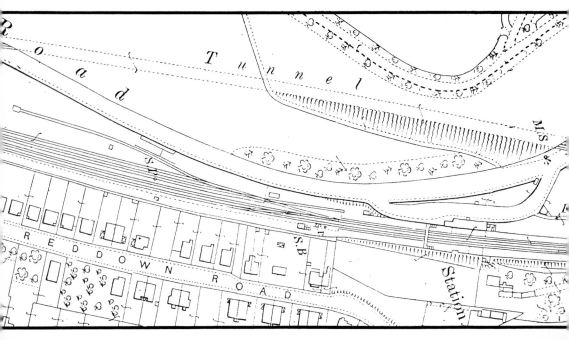

47. The name was changed to "Coulsdon East" on 9th July 1923 and was amended, more logically, to "South" three weeks later. The lattice footbridge remains in use in 1988 but the down platform shelter has been replaced by a fully glazed structure. (Lens of Sutton)

48. The co-acting signals are off as H class 0–4–4T no. A546 waits to depart with an up train on 28th May 1927. At most stations, oil for the signal lamps was kept in an iron shed remote from the main buildings. (H.C. Casserley)

49. After the closure of Coulsdon South Box on 2nd May 1937, Star Bridge Signals became the only intermediate box between Coulsdon North and Merstham. It was closed on 26th February 1983 and is seen with typical SER sash windows on 20th April 1976. (J. Scrace)

50. Diesel no. 33006 climbs the 1 in 264 gradient under Star Bridge on the same day, with the 14.55 from Norwood Yard to Merstham Sidings. The train has passed under the Quarry Line (the bridge in the background) and is approaching Merstham Tunnel, which is 1 mile 71 yards long. The signal box is just visible, on the left. (J. Scrace)

MERSTHAM

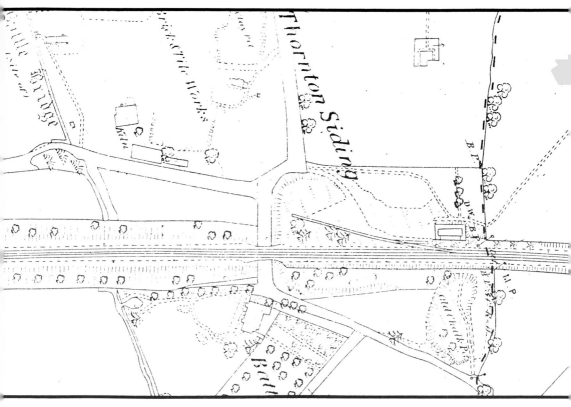

From 1st December 1841 until 1st October 1843, the station was situated one mile south of the present site and thus rather remote from the village. A siding was retained there and shows on this 1877 map. It was still shown on the 1933 edition, along with the station house.

51. A station was opened in the present position on 4th October 1844 and is seen here just prior to rebuilding in 1905. This southward view shows the signal box before it was moved further north and the platforms in the process of reconstruction.
(D. Cullum collection)

52. A new and covered footbridge was erected closer to the station house. The bridge retained its roof in 1988, but had lost its glazing, whereas the down waiting room survived, looking rather comical devoid of its canopy. (Lens of Sutton)

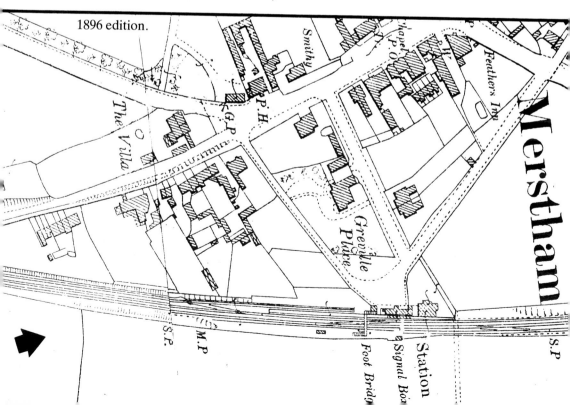

1896 edition.

53. A 4CIG unit heads the 16.28 semi-fast service to Brighton on 28th August 1974, as the rear coaches pass over the then recently built bridge over the M25. On the right is the span carrying the Quarry Line over it. The siding was used for the transfer of motorway construction materials in 1971-74. A number of sidings were laid here during WWII and were used to stable goods trains when Redhill was too congested. (J. Scrace)

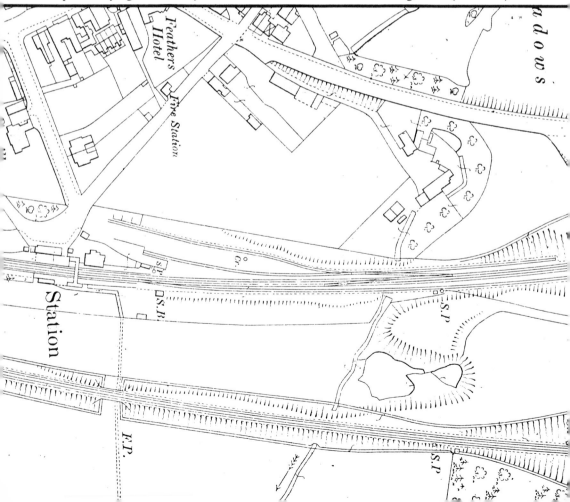

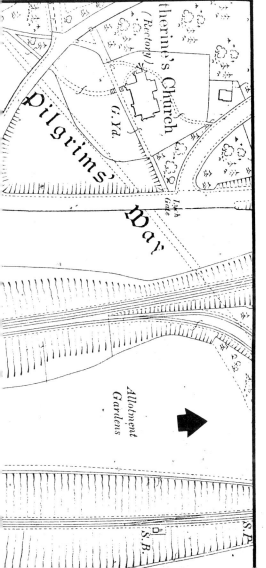

54. Described as neo-Georgian, the pebble-dash and casement windows must have given a modern impression to the Edwardians, who had inherited so much brick and sash fenestration from the Victorians. A smart appearance was still presented when photographed in 1975. (J. Scrace)

The 1913 map includes the new modest goods yard and also the nearby Quarry Line. The third line north from the signal box ran to the Greystone Limeworks and was known as Peters or Ashcombe siding. The siding crossed the Quarry Line on a bridge, now demolished, to reach the quarry which is seen in the background of photograph no. 75.

SOUTHERN RAILWAY.
Available on the DATE of issue ONLY.
This ticket is issued subject to the Regulations
& Conditions stated in the Company's Time
Tables & Bills.
HAYWARDS Heath
TO
PURLEY P
THIRD CLASS.
3/1 Fare. 3/1

6908 6908

HOLMETHORPE SIDING

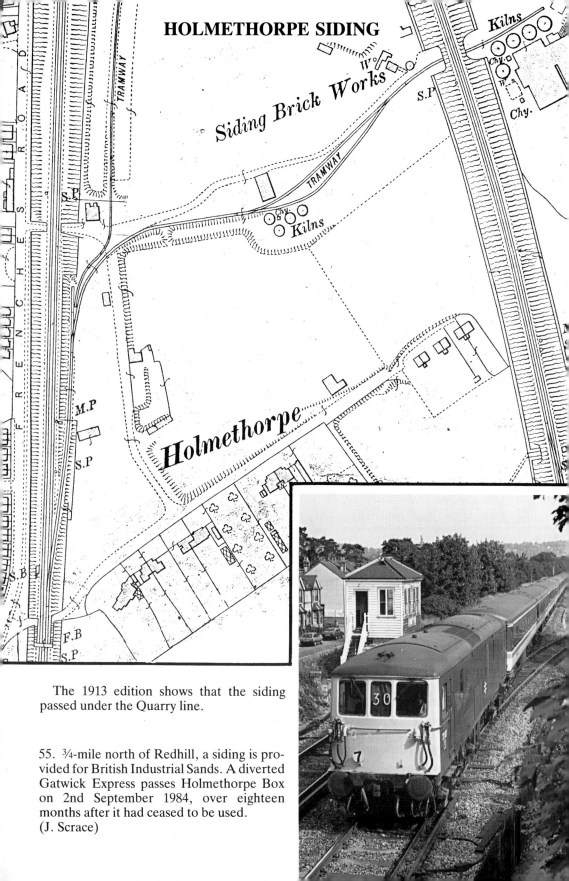

The 1913 edition shows that the siding passed under the Quarry line.

55. ¾-mile north of Redhill, a siding is provided for British Industrial Sands. A diverted Gatwick Express passes Holmethorpe Box on 2nd September 1984, over eighteen months after it had ceased to be used. (J. Scrace)

56. A telephoto lens enables us to look down the industrial siding on 26th February 1984, as a 4VEP unit passes the redundant signal post. The chalk mass of the North Downs gives way to exposures of clay and sand in this vicinity. The agreement for a private siding here was dated 1867. (P.G. Barnes)

57. Sentinel shunter *Gervasse* gives a modicum of banking assistance to class 4 2–6–0 no. 76057 on 23rd November 1957, as it returns towards the main line. *Gervasse* was sent to the Kent & East Sussex Railway upon retirement. In 1988 two Barclay diesels were in use and about 300 tons of sand were despatched daily to Warrington, for making glass. (J.J. Smith)

REDHILL

58. The first L&B station was south of the junction, while the first SER station was to the east. They were both closed in 1844 when this elegant station was opened by the SER, on the present site, for the use of both companies' trains. It was known as Reigate until 1849 and as Reigate Junction until it was rebuilt in 1858. The name Redhill Junction was applied until 1929, when "Junction" was dropped. In the early years, it was often spelled "Red Hill". (Lens of Sutton)

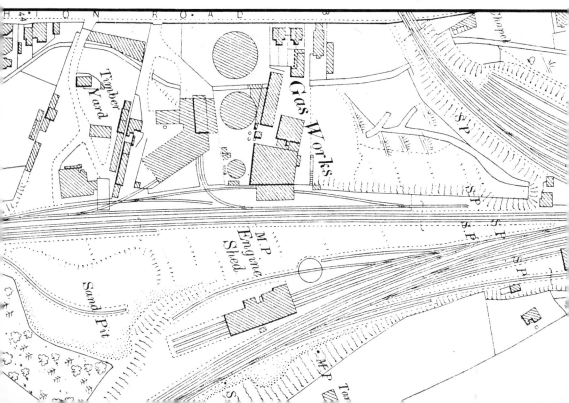

The 1896 map shows the position of the locomotive shed and the 45ft. turntable, which was later replaced by one of 65ft. diameter. The first SER station was in this vicinity.

59. A photograph from about 1890 shows an up LBSCR van train passing the distinctive SER signals, with their white dots and separate coloured spectacle glasses. The line to Reigate curves to the right, this side of No. 2 or B Box. (J.R.W. Kirkby collection)

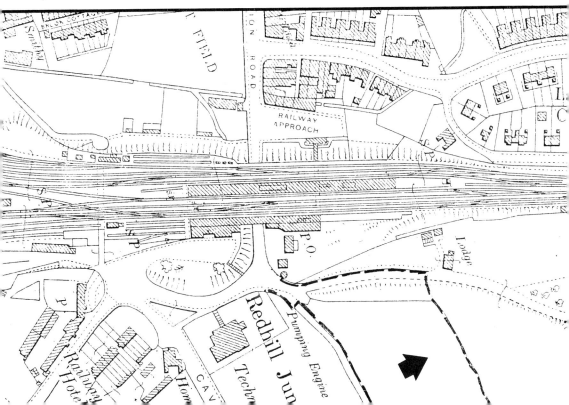

60. The view of the north end of the station, in about 1909, includes no. 1 or A Box and a glimpse over the town. The up passenger train is passing a fine variety of wagons. There was no up bay platform at that time. (Pamlin Prints)

61. Ex-LBSCR class D1 no. 276 stands on the up through line, shortly after the grouping and before being renumbered. The photograph is marked "new electric stock for SECR section en route for Lancing". It would probably receive its trailer coaches there. (O.J. Morris/E. Jackson collection)

62. Another post-grouping photograph shows an ex-LBSCR class B1 arriving with a London Bridge to Eastbourne train, while ex-SECR class F1 no. A89 waits to reverse onto the down line to reach the shed. (J.R.W. Kirkby collection)

63. A class I3 runs in on the down main with a Pullman train, probably destined for Gatwick Racecourse. The access to the up bay is seen by No. 1 Box. The siding is adjacent to the Post Office and conveys considerable mail traffic. (Lens of Sutton)

64. The value of through roads at junction stations is demonstrated as Q class no. 30538 passes through with the Norwood Junction to Horsham freight on 8th August 1959. To reduce congestion during the evacuation of Dunkirk, local passenger services were suspended for over a week. (J. Scrace)

65. A diesel shunter stands with vans at the Post Office platform, as 2 BILs pass the rebuilt A Box on 4th July 1969. They form the 16.27 from Littlehampton which called at all stations to Gatwick Airport, then East Croydon and Victoria. (J. Scrace)

66. B Box was in the divergence of the Brighton and Guildford lines and controlled a varied array of semaphore signals, until superseded by Three Bridges Panel Box on 12th May 1985. This is the west elevation in 1982. (J. Scrace)

67. Redhill is still an important freight centre, particularly for minerals and oil distribution. Nos. 73103 and 73123 are seen with the 0310 Cliff Brett Marine to Purley train on 28th August 1985. Passengers use a subway – an endless conveyor for moving and sorting mailbags passes across the bridge. (J. Scrace)

REDHILL SHED

69. Looking west over the Tonbridge lines with the North Downs in the distance, we see the three road shed which was finished in 1928. Beyond it is a small building containing a wheel drop and at a higher level is the coal stage. The gas works buildings are beyond, in this June 1958 view. (J. Scrace)

68. Tonbridge, Reading and Gatwick Airport DMUs mainly use the up loop (platforms 1a and 1b) – one is seen leaving on 31st August 1987. On 12th December 1987, passenger facilities improved with the opening of a bus station north of the roundabout and rebuilding of the down side commenced. (J. Scrace)

70. N class no. 31857 is turned on 18th October 1963 – one man pushing and the other operating the gearing. A van body displays LBSC – 40 years on! The shed officially closed in January 1965 but locomotives continued to stand there. Most of the buildings were demolished but DMUs continue to be berthed on the site. (J. Scrace)

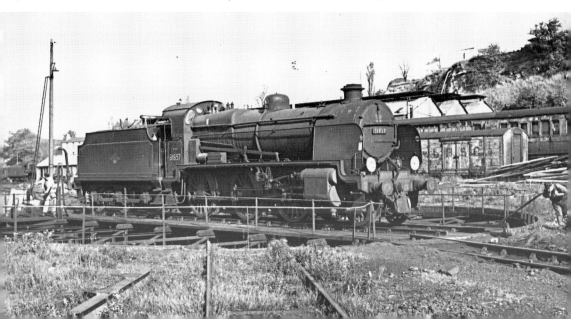

71. The 6½-mile stationless "Redhill bypass" is on the west side of the old route on leaving Coulsdon North and, after 1½ miles, crosses it on this skew bridge. Class H1 no. 39 speeds south with the all Pullman *Southern Belle*, precursor of the better known *Brighton Belle*. (Lens of Sutton)

72. The skew bridge is known as Star Bridge, after the nearby Star Inn on the A23. J class 4–6–2T no. B325, formerly *Abergavenny*, climbs the North Downs en route for Brighton. In the foreground is an engineer's siding – chalk falls are not uncommon. The siding later gave access to a sub-station. (J.R.W. Kirkby collection)

73. Perhaps more aptly described as the "Quarried Line", steps lead down the rock face to Star Lane Signal Box. This view is northwards, the engineer's siding being visible in the distance. (Lens of Sutton)

74. Star Lane Intermediate Box, photographed in 1973, remained in use until 19th November 1978. Other nearby boxes closed in 1932 – Cane Hill to the north and Quarry and Worsted Green boxes to the south. Until 1954, the line in the vicinity of Cane Hill Asylum was roofed over to "avoid more distress to the inmates" and was known to all as "The Covered Way". (E. Wilmshurst)

←

75. Class B4X no. B70 races south, down the in 264 gradient which follows the 1 mile 353 yard long tunnel on this route. In the background is the quarry of the Greystone Limeworks and Quarry Signal Box. S.C. Nash collection)

76. Looking south on 2nd September 1984, we witness the Gatwick Airport to Manchester service approaching, as a Gatwick Express runs south. The middle coaches of the up train are crossing the M25; Merstham station is on the right and the footbridges once spanned five sidings. They have both since been demolished. (P.G. Barnes)

78. An Eastbourne to Colne train swings away from the old route as it approaches Redhill Tunnel on the Quarry Line, on 18th July 1959. The locomotive is LMS class 5 no. 45426. On the extreme right, a connection from the turntable joins the down Redhill line. Ten sidings were provided in the goods yard, one of which ran through the goods shed. (J. Scrace)

77. Both routes pass through long tunnels in chalk but the Quarry Line has an additional tunnel, 649 yards long, through sand. The 16.32 Victoria to Brighton emerges from it on 23rd September 1985, while diesel locomotives stand at the end of the former Redhill steam depot. (J. Scrace)

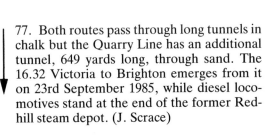

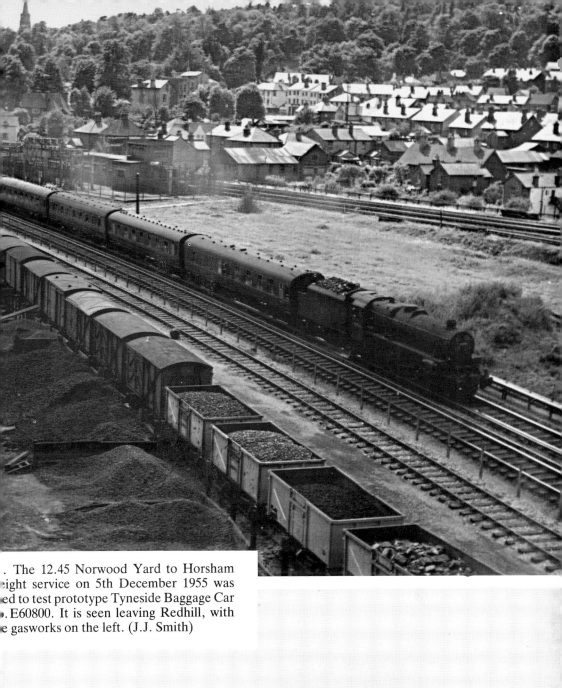

. The 12.45 Norwood Yard to Horsham
ight service on 5th December 1955 was
ed to test prototype Tyneside Baggage Car
. E60800. It is seen leaving Redhill, with
e gasworks on the left. (J.J. Smith)

80. Looking north on 17th March 1987, we see the point of divergence of the Quarry Line, opposite Earlswood Box. The train is carrying a welcoming party for the President of Nigeria, who was arriving at Gatwick Airport, and is hauled by electro-diesel no. 73142. Known as Earlswood Junction until 1932, the signal box replaced a smaller one when the Quarry Line was opened. It ceased to function on 2nd July 1983. The original LBSCR goods yard had been located behind the box. (J. Scrace)

→

81. The junction was remodelled to reduce maintenance and raise speed restrictions - note the 90 mph sign. A 3-car DMU from Gatwick Airport to Reading passes eight coaches bound for Portsmouth via Horsham as an express hurries towards the Quarry Line. Tankers of heating oil stand on the former gasworks line and a rake of wagons stand in the ballast dump. (P.G. Barnes)

London Brighton & South Coast Railway.

Midhurst to

RED HILL

EARLSWOOD

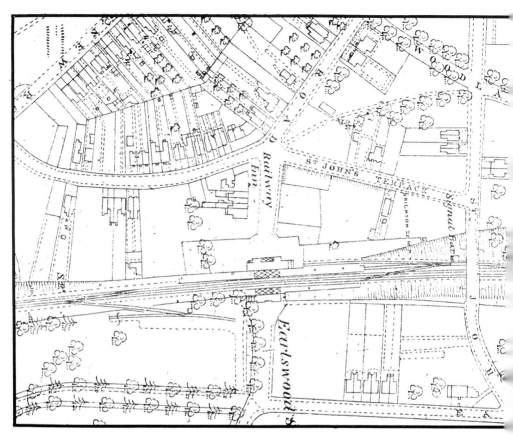

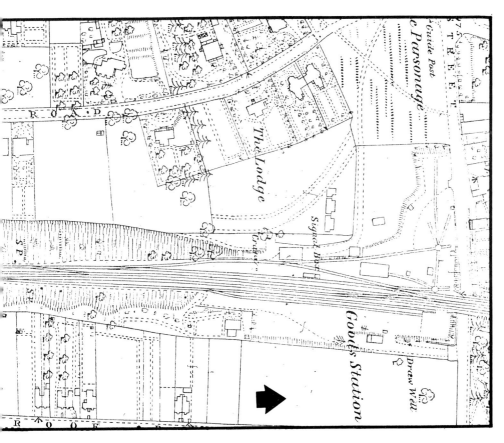

The 1872 edition shows the position of the first station which opened in August 1868. The "Goods Station" is the site of L&B Redhill station, in use until 1844.

82. This southward view illustrates the station after rebuilding in 1900-05, following the quadrupling of the tracks. The main buildings were erected further west to make way for the additional lines and a subway was provided. (Lens of Sutton)

83. Class A 0–6–0T no. 83 *Earlswood* stands behind the Station Box which found itself at the north end of the new island platform during the alterations, having previously been on the west of the double track. The siding eventually became part of the down local line and St. Johns Road bridge received another span. (D.E. Wallis collection)

84. An up express rushes through behind class H1 4–4–2 no. 38 in about 1910. The siding on the left was used for coal for Earlswood Asylum for Idiots, later renamed the Royal Earlswood Institution. Two other sidings were provided in the cutting on the right. (Lens of Sutton)

The 1913 map shows the position of Earlswood Station and Junction Boxes. The goods yard had become a timber yard by then.

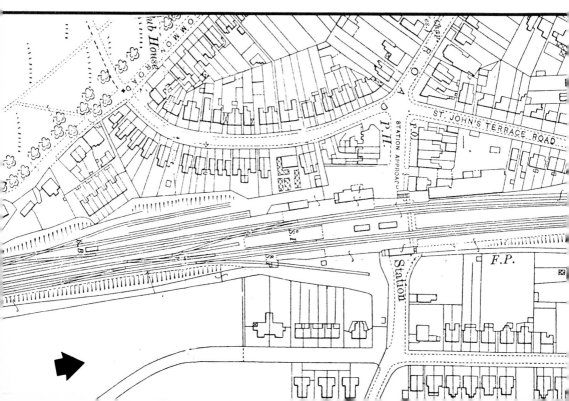

85. Looking north from the south end of the up local platform in 1958, we see the gate across the private siding, which was lifted in 1964. A signal box at the country end of this platform was in use until 1932. (D. Cullum)

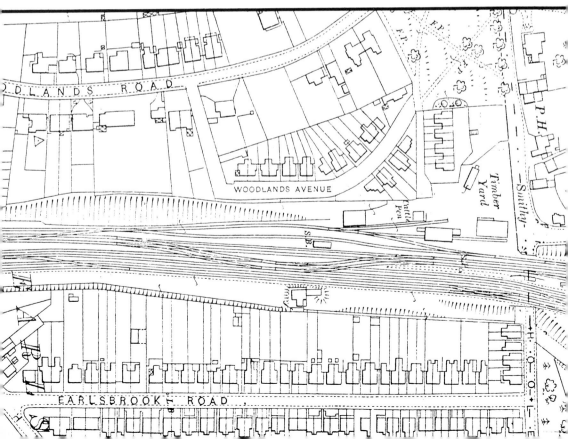

86. The up side buildings in 1958, still bore a motif showing AD1905 and 30 years later continued to support a platform canopy. By then the island platform only had a small glazed shelter and trains only called in the peak hours. (D. Cullum)

London Brighton & South Coast Railway.

Forest Row to

Earlswood

SALFORDS

57. Opened as Salfords Halt on 8th October 1915, its use was restricted to workers to and from local factories – principally Mullards. During the first world war special trains ran from East Croydon calling at Purley, Merstham, Redhill and Earlswood, another from Three Bridges calling at Horley. The first, the only LBSCR train to call at Merstham, stabled at Three Bridges, the second at Earlswood for return in the evening. From October 1922 these were replaced by a Horsham Rail Motor running to Redhill and back, morning and evening. This is the down platform in February 1950, after it had been lengthened. (Lens of Sutton)

The initial design of the halt is superimposed on the 1913 edition.

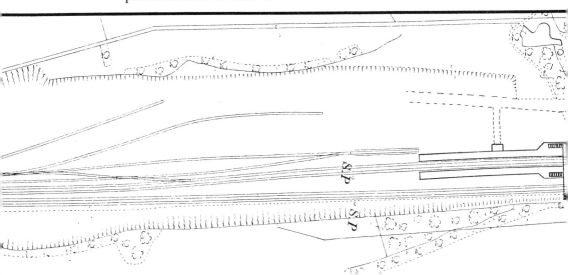

89. Holiday traffic between the South Coast and the North of England was particularly heavy in the 1950s. This is the 2.15 pm from Brighton to Manchester, headed by ex-LMS no. 45426 on 22nd August 1959. The train had originated at Eastbourne at 1.31 pm. (J.J. Smith)

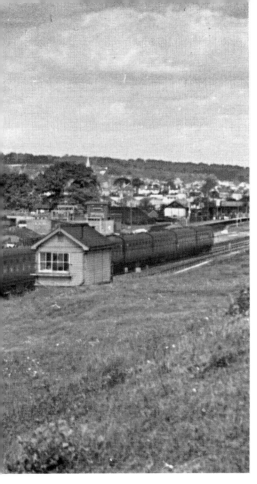

88. From December 1925 the 6.20 am and 4.10 pm (not Sats) Brighton to London Bridge made unadvertised stops at Salfords Halt. All these trains were withdrawn on electrification in July 1932 but a Horsham motor continued to run to Redhill and back in the morning for fish, mails and parcels as well as passengers. From 1938 this was replaced by the 7.10 am electric Redhill to Portsmouth Harbour. Salfords Halt came into full public service on 17th July 1932 and ceased to be a "halt" from 1 January 1935. Sidings into a coal yard and a timber yard can be seen behind the Perry Barr to Brighton excursion, which was hauled by LMS designed class 5 no. 45395 on 24th August 1957. (S.C. Nash)

90. On 23rd August 1959, ex-LBSCR K class 2–6–0 no. 32342 hauls a special of 22 tank cars from Hoo Junction to Three Bridges. They were probably bound for the depot at Rowfant, having run via Tonbridge. (J.J. Smith)

→

91. No. 33207 proceeds north on 24th June 1978, its train of empties passing tank wagons standing by the aviation fuel storage tanks. They were erected in 1969 and dismantled in 1987, fuel now arriving direct from the refinery by pipeline. Aggregates from Cliffe, in Kent, were still sent by rail in 1988 to the Marinex terminal, visible on the right. (J. Scrace)

HORLEY

92. The first station was opened with the line. This is the second one, built in about 1883 and viewed north from the Victoria Road level crossing. Both had loops and centre through roads, as at Redhill. Station Road level crossing is close to the signal in the distance. This photograph, from about 1895, shows a massive water tank on the down platform which was required to supply locomotives standing in the platform loops. (Lens of Sutton)

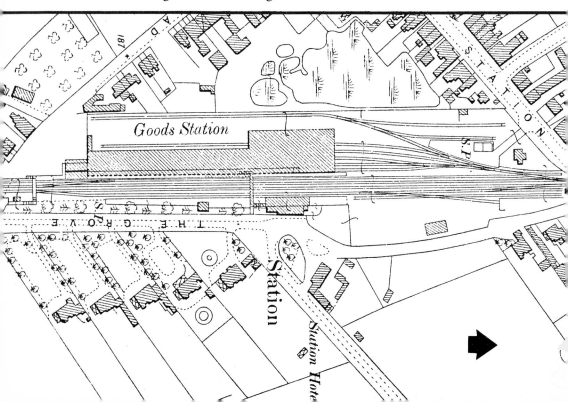

93. A closer look at the Station Road crossing in about 1903 shows how un-level it was. Both crossings were eliminated prior to quadrupling, as part of a scheme to eliminate all crossings between London and Brighton – a far sighted ideal. (Lens of Sutton)

The 1896 cartographer refers to a "Goods Station". This was also used for storage of rolling stock and as a granary at different times. Sidings are shown alongside the brewery and into the gasworks.

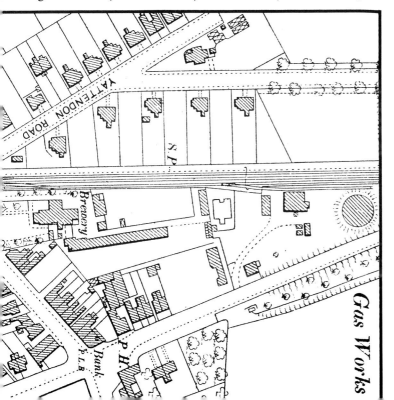

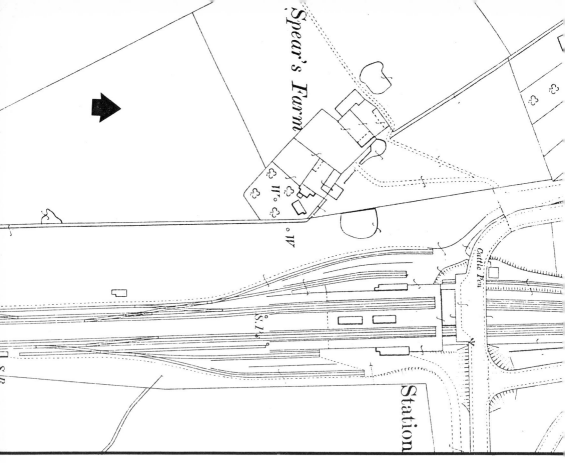

94. A Craven 0–6–0 shunts engines awaiting scrapping. The photograph was taken from the cattle dock in about 1895 and shows the station and goods shed in the background.
(Lens of Sutton)

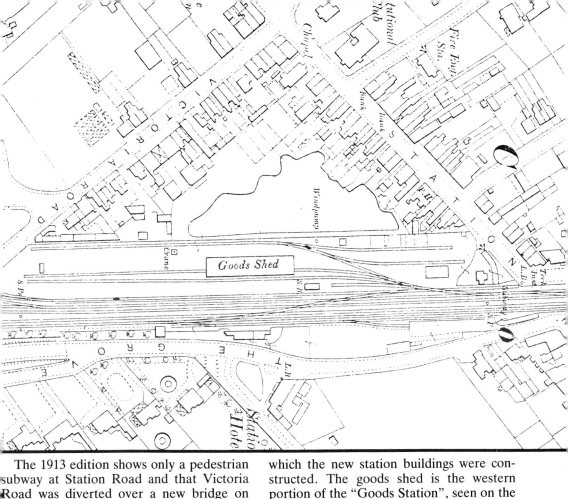

The 1913 edition shows only a pedestrian subway at Station Road and that Victoria Road was diverted over a new bridge on which the new station buildings were constructed. The goods shed is the western portion of the "Goods Station", seen on the 1896 map.

95. An interesting transitional view shows South Box and the recently constructed ramp up to the new road bridge. The siding on the left leads to the locomotive scrap yard, which was in use from 1884, until 1903. The train is bound for Eastbourne behind a class B4 4–4–0. (Lens of Sutton)

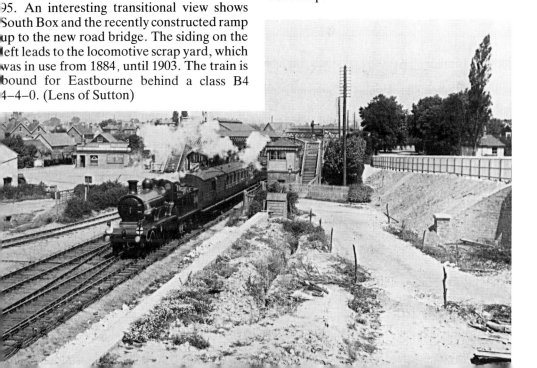

96. The new well-appointed station came
into use on 31st December 1905. The generous facilities were justified by the population
growth – 2,300 in 1881, 6,000 in 1921 and
16,000 in 1961. They no doubt contributed to
it. (E. Jackson collection)

97. Horley was again the location chosen for
locomotive scrapping, in 1949-50. A class D1
meets its fate as class U1 no. 31907 passes by
with a Shoeburyness to Hove excursion on
4th March 1950. (S.C. Nash)

98. No. 31734, an ex-SECR D class 4–4–0, runs on the up local line with the 9.25 am Hastings to Birkenhead service. This train had to reverse at Eastbourne, Brighton and Redhill. Horley B Box is on the left and the former scrapyard is on the right. (S.C. Nash)

99. The spacious and well-lit station retains most of its Edwardian features – only the down main canopy has gone. The last slip coach arrived here in April 1927, being shed from the 5.05 pm London Bridge to Eastbourne train and destined for Forest Row. (J. Scrace)

GATWICK RACECOURSE

100. The station was opened in March 1891, the owner of the racecourse paying the LBSCR £5000 towards its cost. Here we see the south end of the platforms, soon after the completion of quadrupling in 1907. (Pamlin Prints)

101. This is the signalman's view north in 1931. Conductor rails are in place ready for electric services to commence in the following year. The sign in the foreground is at the bottom of the steps of the second footbridge. (Late E. Wallis)

102. Trains only stopped on race days, but not the *Brighton Belle* which is seen speeding south on 17th March 1956. We see two of three five-car sets reserved for this prestigious service, which was withdrawn on 30th April 1972. The buildings were demolished to make way for the new Gatwick Airport station, a mile north of its predecessor. Racing had ceased years earlier. (J.J. Smith)

The 1913 edition emphasises the close proximity of the grand stand, band stand and paddock to the station. Between them flows a stream which joined the River Mole on the north side of the course.

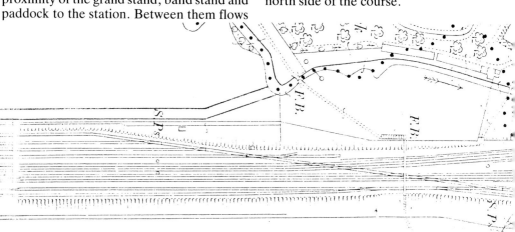

Use of the up sidings for staging empty wagons destined for the Midland and Great Northern Railways via Battersea ceased in 1925. During WWI, the sidings were used extensively for staging traffic to and from the port of Littlehampton.

No.2 TRAINS FOR LONDON BRIDGE AND INTERMEDIATE STATIONS

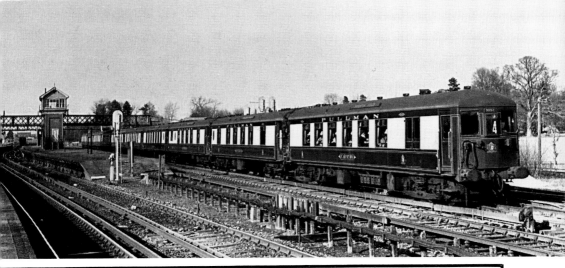

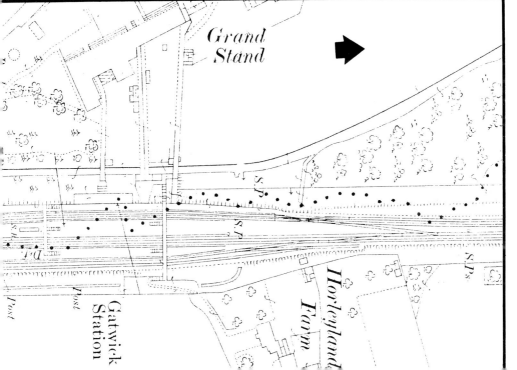

Grand Stand

Gatwick Station

Horleyland Farm

GATWICK AIRPORT

103. After years of uncertainty, the Government decided that the old airport should close in 1956 to allow a new one to be constructed on its site. This was to be combined with the site of the former racecourse. Station reconstruction is seen on 14th November 1957. (British Rail)

104. The sidings at the south end of the station, which formerly housed race specials, were electrified to take terminating trains from Victoria. The 17.14 Newhaven Harbour to Victoria boat train passes under a flight path on 9th May 1963, hauled by ex-SR electric locomotive no. 20001. (J. Scrace)

105. A siding for aviation fuel was in use from 1969 until 1971, when the traffic was transferred to Salfords. No. 1685 leaves another short-lived siding at the north end of the station on 26th April 1973. This one was in use in 1971-74 for the unloading of motorway construction stone, brought mainly from Westbury. (J. Scrace)

106. A Bognor Regis train departs from platform 2 on 26th April 1973. The new luggage lifts are visible, as is the old signal box which remained in use until 29th April 1978. Trains from every Sussex town now call at this station which serves the world's second busiest airport. It is used by over 100 airlines and handles more than 19 million passengers per annum. (J. Scrace)

107. 4 COR units were used regularly on the main line, to such destinations as Ore and Portsmouth Harbour. The only preserved unit is seen being hauled by no. 73142 on 5th September 1986. It was in transit from the Nene Valley Railway at Peterborough to the former Pullman Works at Brighton. Behind the road embankment, a driverless automatic railway runs out to a new air terminal. (S.C. Nash)

109. Part of Cotland Farm was licensed as an aerodrome on 30th July 1930 and in 1934 Airports Ltd agreed to pay the SR £3000 towards the cost of a station. The SR was reluctant to participate in a scheme that would make inroads into their lucrative European traffic, specially as they had recently formed Railway Air Services Ltd., jointly with the GWR. This is a 1956 southward view of the station, which was of standard SR design. (J.J. Smith)

108. Tinsley Green was the name given to the first airport station when it opened on 30th September 1935, it being changed to Gatwick Airport on 1st June 1936. The signal box was closed on 5th June 1932 but the name is still displayed at the lineside to locate some crossovers. The box had been located beyond the bridge in the next picture. (Late E. Wallis)

110. Looking north in 1956, the proximity of the airport is obvious. Airwork Ltd. took over the British Airways' hangar in 1938 for maintenance of RAF and, later, commercial aircraft. (J.J. Smith)

111. The station was linked to the terminal building by means of a well-lit subway. Unfortunately it was prone to flooding and mailbags were transported on a make-shift pontoon. Illuminated display cabinets were provided for the West End stores – in reality they were used by some traders from Horley. This photograph was taken on 26th May 1958, two days before the station closed. (E. Wilmshurst)

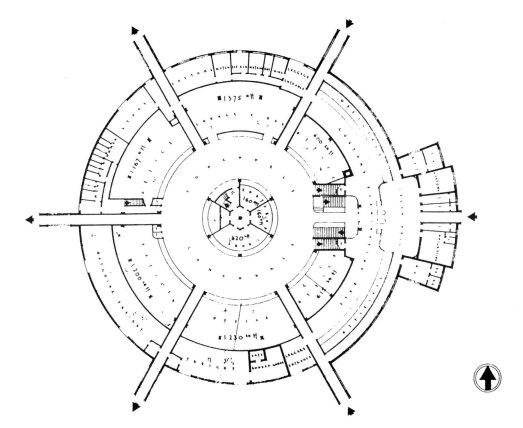

A revolutionary new circular design was used for the terminal buildings – an idea not copied for another twenty years. The ground floor plan shows the positions of radiating telescopic passages, which were pushed out to waiting aeroplanes – another unique innovation. International services commenced on 18th May 1936, with a weekday service to Malmo calling at Amsterdam, Hamburg and Copenhagen with an hourly service to Paris, reduced to two flights on Sundays. British Airways also operated seasonally to Ryde and Cowes, in conjunction with the SR. Owing to waterlogging of the grass runways, operations were transferred to Croydon Airport early in 1937. Gatwick became a joke associated with sea-planes and continued a perilous existence until being taken over for military purposes in WWII. Commercial flying and a full train service was restored in 1946. Two trains per hour each way called – the Brighton semi-fast and stopping services. The building was originally known as London South (Gatwick) Airport Martello Air Station but was quickly dubbed The Beehive. It can still be seen from the main line. (Sussex Industrial Archæology Society)

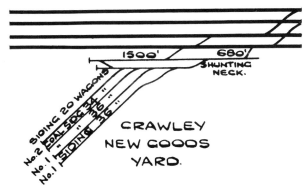

CRAWLEY NEW GOODS YARD.

Associated with the Crawley New Town development, a new goods yard was brought into use in 1969, remote from Crawley station. The control diagram shows the sidings at a large angle to the main line – in reality it is 30°. They have been used to serve coal concentration depots and aggregate terminals as well as a large warehouse, and most were still in use in 1988.

THREE BRIDGES

112. Opened with the main line, the station was called "Crawley" until 1848, when a station on the then new Horsham branch was opened closer to the town. A Victoria to Hastings express is seen entering the station in 1898. (J.R.W. Kirkby collection)

113. Another view before quadrupling in 1907 includes the first locomotive shed, on the extreme left. The covered up loop was mainly used by branch line trains to Horsham, while the partially covered bay platform on the right was used by trains on the East Grinstead branch, after that line opened on 9th July 1855. (Lens of Sutton)

114. This is the shed seen in the previous picture, the locomotives being class D 0–4–2T no. 275 *Cranleigh* and "Terrier" 0–6–0T no. 59 *Cheam*. Two locomotive sheds and two turntables were later provided, beyond the divergence of the Horsham line. (S.C. Nash collection)

115. Driver Thomas Chappell poses proudly with his two sons on King Edward VII's Coronation Day in 1902. The class C2 no. 440 was on stand-by duty for the royal train. Central Box, in the background, was taken out of use in 1932. (L. Chappell collection)

116. The view from North Box in 1923 shows the arrangement of tracks after quadrupling. This took place in 1907 northwards and south to Balcombe, in 1910. The basic layout is the same today, the platforms being numbered 1 to 5, from west to east. (Late E. Wallis)

117. Unlike Central Box which was on a brick base, North Box was entirely of timber construction. Like South Box, this one was taken out of use in 1932. (Late E. Wallis)

118. This photograph was taken from Central Box, which was superseded by an SR style flat-roofed box in 1952. It was located on the extreme left of this picture and was demolished in 1986. The goods yard closed on 4th May 1964. (Lens of Sutton)

119. The 1841 station buildings, on the left, were given an additional storey in 1867. Almost all of the structures seen on platform 5 in this 1961 view have been demolished, a WH Smith wholesale warehouse and a signalling centre having been erected in their place. The only exception is the small canopy, seen under the main one, which is still supported by old double-head rails, as is part of the roof over platforms 3 and 4. (D. Cullum)

 The 1874 map of the station is included in our *Branch Lines to East Grinstead* and the 1911 edition appears in our *Three Bridges to Brighton* album. Other photographs of the route are to be found in Peter Hay's *Steaming through Surrey, Steaming through East Sussex* and *Steaming through West Sussex*.

120. The signalling centre contains seven linked panels operated by seven signalmen simultaneously. The area controlled is bounded by Norbury, Penge West, Waddon, Upper Warlingham, Godstone, Faygate, Falmer and Aldrington. This is the first panel, with the London Bridge and Victoria lines on the left. Together with a similar installation near Clapham Junction, the centre controls one of the busiest and most remunerative railway routes in Britain. (P.G. Barnes)

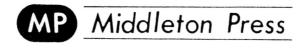

MP *Middleton Press*

Easebourne Lane, Midhurst, West Sussex, GU29 9AZ
☎ Midhurst (073 081) 3169

BRANCH LINES
BRANCH LINES TO MIDHURST
BRANCH LINES TO HORSHAM
BRANCH LINES TO EAST GRINSTEAD
BRANCH LINES TO ALTON
BRANCH LINE TO HAYLING
BRANCH LINE TO SOUTHWOLD
BRANCH LINE TO TENTERDEN
BRANCH LINES TO NEWPORT
BRANCH LINES TO TUNBRIDGE WELLS
BRANCH LINE TO SWANAGE
BRANCH LINES AROUND GOSPORT
BRANCH LINES TO LONGMOOR
BRANCH LINES TO LYME REGIS
BRANCH LINES **AROUND** MIDHURST
BRANCH LINE TO FAIRFORD

SOUTH COAST RAILWAYS
BRIGHTON TO WORTHING
WORTHING TO CHICHESTER
CHICHESTER TO PORTSMOUTH
BRIGHTON TO EASTBOURNE
RYDE TO VENTNOR
EASTBOURNE TO HASTINGS
PORTSMOUTH TO SOUTHAMPTON
HASTINGS TO ASHFORD*
SOUTHAMPTON TO BOURNEMOUTH
ASHFORD TO DOVER

COUNTRY RAILWAY ROUTES
BOURNEMOUTH TO EVERCREECH JUNCTION
READING TO GUILDFORD

SOUTHERN MAIN LINES
WOKING TO PORTSMOUTH
HAYWARDS HEATH TO SEAFORD
EPSOM TO HORSHAM
CRAWLEY TO LITTLEHAMPTON
THREE BRIDGES TO BRIGHTON
WATERLOO TO WOKING
VICTORIA TO EAST CROYDON
TONBRIDGE TO HASTINGS
EAST CROYDON TO THREE BRIDGES

STEAMING THROUGH
STEAMING THROUGH KENT
STEAMING THROUGH EAST HANTS
STEAMING THROUGH EAST SUSSEX
STEAMING THROUGH SURREY
STEAMING THROUGH WEST SUSSEX

OTHER BOOKS
MIDHURST TOWN – THEN & NOW
EAST GRINSTEAD – THEN & NOW
THE MILITARY DEFENCE OF WEST SUSSEX
WEST SUSSEX WATERWAYS
SURREY WATERWAYS
BATTLE OVER PORTSMOUTH
A City at war in 1940
SUSSEX POLICE FORCES

OTHER RAILWAY BOOKS
WAR ON THE LINE
(Reprint of the SR history in World War II)
GARRAWAY FATHER AND SON
(Biography - includes LNER, Talyllyn and Festiniog Railways)

*Video also available. Details from
M.P. Videos, 11 Park Crescent, Midhurst,
West Sussex GU29 9ED.*